What Does a Wrench Do?

by Robin Nelson

first step nonfiction

Lerner Publications Company · Minneapolis

What tool is this?

It is a wrench.

Tools help us do jobs.

Wrenches make jobs easier.

Wrenches help turn things.

Wrenches tighten **nuts**.
Nuts hold **bolts** in place.

There are many kinds of wrenches.

This wrench has **jaws**. The jaws hold things we want to turn.

9

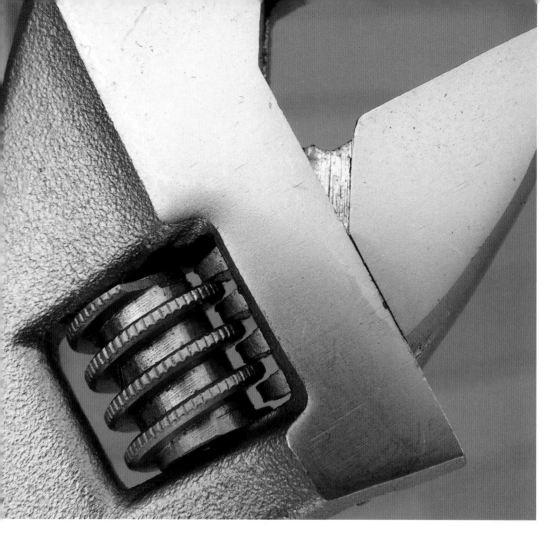

Some wrenches have a **knob**.

The knob opens or closes
the jaws.

This is a wrench's handle.

We push or pull the handle
to turn the jaws.

A wrench can help tighten
a pipe.

A wrench can help loosen
a nut and bolt.

You can use a wrench to fix your bike.

What else can you do with a wrench?

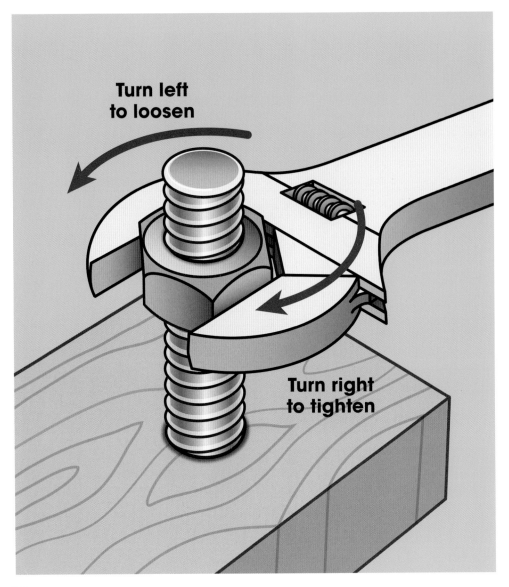

Turn left to loosen

Turn right to tighten

Wrenches Are Levers

Wrenches are simple machines. They are **levers**. A lever is a strong bar that is used to move something. Place a nut on a bolt. Use the jaws on a wrench to tightly hold the nut. Pull the handle to turn the nut around the bolt. The wrench acts as a lever. The wrench makes it easier to tighten or loosen the nut.

Safety First

 Ask a grown-up to help before using any tools.

 Wear safety glasses to protect your eyes.

 Roll up your sleeves. Tuck in your shirt. Tie back your hair. Remove any jewelry that might get in the way.

 Carry a wrench with the top down and away from your body.

Never run with a tool in your hand.

 Be careful not to pinch your fingers.

 Put the wrench away when you are done with your job.

Glossary

 bolts – thick pieces of metal that hold two things together

 jaws – the parts of a wrench that hold on to something we want to turn

 knob – a metal part on a wrench that opens or closes the jaws

 levers – strong bars that are used to move something

 nuts – small metal pieces with a hole that turn around a bolt

Index

Expand learning beyond the printed book. Download free, complementary educational resources for this book from our website, www.lerneresource.com.

The images in this book are used with the permission of: © Todd Strand/Independent Picture Service, pp. 2, 3, 11, 12, 13, 16, 17; © mihalec/Shutterstock.com, p. 4; © Jose Luis Pelaez Inc/Blend Images/Getty Images, p. 5; © Frank Gaglione/Digital Vision/Getty Images, p. 6; © Laurent Hamels/PhotoAlto Agency RF Collections/Getty Images, pp. 7, 22; © Peter Galbraith/Dreamstime.com, p. 8; © Ronen/Shutterstock.com, pp. 9, 22; © Dino/Shutterstock.com, pp. 10, 22; © sima/Shutterstock.com, p. 14; © Thinkstock Images/Comstock Images/Getty Images, p. 15; © Laura Westlund/Independent Picture Service, pp. 18, 20, 21, 22.

Front cover: © iStockphoto.com/Andrew Horwitz.

Main body text set in ITC Avant Garde Gothic Std Medium 21/25.
Typeface provided by Adobe Systems.

Lerner Publications Company
A division of Lerner Publishing Group, Inc.
241 First Avenue North
Minneapolis, MN 55401 U.S.A.

Website address: www.lernerbooks.com

Library of Congress Cataloging-in-Publication Data

Nelson, Robin, 1971–
　　What does a wrench do? / by Robin Nelson.
　　　p.　cm. — (First step nonfiction–tools at work)
　　Includes index.
　　ISBN 978–0–7613–8977–4 (lib. bdg. : alk. paper)
　　　1. Wrenches—Juvenile literature. I. Title.
　TJ1201.W8N45 2013
　621.9'72—dc23　　　　　　　　　　　2011039078

Manufactured in the United States of America
1 – CG – 7/15/12